HEALTHY
AND HAPPY

Eating Well

Robyn Hardyman

First published in 2010 by Wayland
Copyright © Wayland 2010

This paperback edition published in 2012
by Wayland

Wayland, 338 Euston Road, London NW1 3BH
Wayland, Level 17/207 Kent Street, Sydney, NSW 2000

British Library Cataloguing in Publication Data
Hardyman, Robyn.
    Eating well. — (Healthy and happy)
    1. Nutrition—Juvenile literature. 2. Food preferences—
    Juvenile literature.
    I. Title II. Series
    613.2-dc22

ISBN 978-0-7502-6798-4

Produced for Wayland by Calcium
Design: Paul Myerscough and Geoff Ward
Editor: Sarah Eason
Editor for Wayland: Joyce Bentley
Illustrations: Geoff Ward
Picture research: Maria Joannou
Consultant: Sue Beck, MSc, BSc

Printed in China

Pic credits: Corbis: Charles Gullung 9; Dreamstime: Monkey Business Images 26; Getty Images: Dorling Kindersley/Will Heap 17; Istockphoto: Marina Kravchenko 18; Rex Features: Image Source 27; Shutterstock: 25, Jacek Chabraszewski 11, Sonya Etchison 14, Gelpi 22, Ilepet 16, John McLaird 24, Stuart Miles 19, Monkey Business Images 4, 5, 6, 21, 23, Xavier Gallego Morell 8, Nayashkova Olga 20, Tobik 2, 13, Denis Vrublevski 7, 32, Whitechild 1, 15, Gautier Willaume 12; Wayland Picture Library 10.

Cover photograph: Shutterstock/Sonya Etchison

Wayland is a division of Hachette Children's Books, an Hachette UK company.

www.hachette.co.uk

Contents

Food is great!

Everyone needs to eat and drink to stay alive. Food gives your body **energy** and **nutrients**, which it needs to work properly. Eating the right types of foods will help to keep you healthy.

HEALTHY HINTS

Try eating a banana an hour before bedtime. Bananas contain a substance which can help you to sleep.

Different-coloured foods contain lots of different nutrients.

A healthy diet

The food you normally eat is called your **diet**. It includes different foods such as bread, fish, fruits and vegetables. You need to eat many types of food to get all the nutrients you need.

Be a food adventurer!

When you eat new foods for the first time, they may taste delicious or may be a bit strange. It's good to keep trying new foods – you might find something you really like.

*Read food labels when you shop. They tell you which **ingredients** are in the food.*

Healthy body

Each nutrient helps your body in different ways. For example, cheese contains calcium, a nutrient that makes bones and teeth strong.

How you use energy

Your body needs energy all the time. You use energy to think, to be active and even when you are resting. The more active you are, the more energy you use.

Eating healthy food gives you lots of energy to enjoy yourself.

Body-building

Your body needs **protein** to grow. Protein comes from food such as cheese, fish and meat. Children need to eat food with lots of protein because their bodies are growing all the time.

Food for health

Some foods, such as vegetables, contain a substance called **fibre**. Fibre pushes food through your body, which helps you to get rid of waste.

*Broccoli contains a **vitamin** that helps cuts to heal.*

It's a fact!

Fruit and vegetables contain vitamins and **minerals**. They help your body to fight disease and stay healthy.

Eating well

You should try to eat three healthy meals each day. These meals are called breakfast, lunch and dinner. It is important to try to eat a variety of foods at each meal.

HEALTHY HINTS

Eat your food slowly. This helps you to chew it properly. Stop eating when you feel full.

If you eat at the same times each day, your body will expect the food and feel hungry.

Breakfast

Breakfast is the first meal of the day. Many people think it is the most important meal. Eating something simple, such as **cereal** with milk, gives you energy for the morning.

Your main meal

Some people have their main meal at lunchtime. Others eat it in the evening, for dinner. Your main meal should include a wide range of healthy foods.

Many families eat their main meal together.

Food groups

There are five main groups of food. You need to eat more foods from some groups than from others. The five main food groups are:

1. Potatoes, bread and cereals such as rice.
2. Fruits and vegetables.
3. Dairy products made from milk.
4. Meat, fish, eggs, beans and nuts.
5. Fatty and sugary foods, such as cakes.

This food plate shows you how much you should eat from the main food groups.

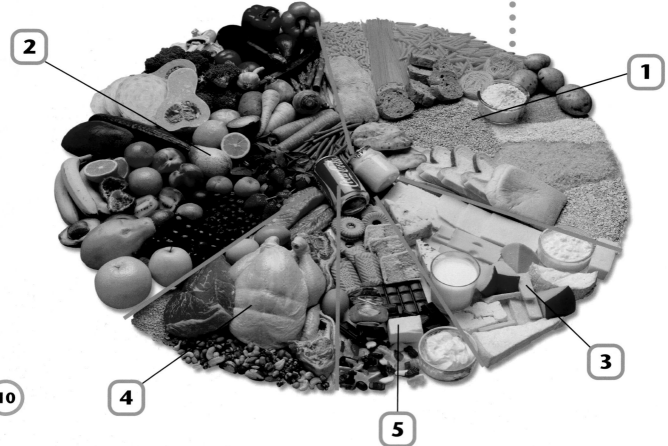

How much of each?

Potatoes, bread and cereals should make up about one-third of your diet. Fruit and vegetables should make up another third.

Dairy food, meat, fish, eggs, beans and nuts should make up the final third of your diet. This leaves room for a just a little **fat** and sugar!

* * *

Vegetarians do not eat meat or fish. They can choose other foods, such as beans or tofu. Pasta with vegetables is a healthy vegetarian meal.

HEALTHY HINTS

The food within each group contains similar nutrients. You can choose what to eat from each group. If you do not like nuts, for example, try eggs or meat instead.

Potatoes and cereals

Cereals and potatoes belong to a food group called carbohydrates. These foods give you energy. Your body uses them for fuel, just like a car uses petrol.

Lots of choice

There are many different ways to cook and eat carbohydrates. Potatoes can be boiled, baked or fried. Bread can be toasted, or eaten as a sandwich. Cereals are grains that include corn, oats, rice and wheat. You can eat cereals with milk for breakfast, or as boiled rice or pasta for a main meal.

Rice is the main food eaten by many people in Asia. It is grown in fields covered with water.

The flour from ground wheat is made into foods such as bread.

Brown or white?

The outer part of the grain has a layer of bran, which is full of fibre. 'Wholemeal' food is made from flour that contains bran. It is good for you because it contains lots of fibre. Brown bread is a type of wholemeal food.

HEALTHY HINTS

Try to avoid white bread, rice and pasta. They do not contain bran. Brown bread, rice and pasta contain bran and are better for you.

Fruits and vegetables

Fruits and vegetables contain many vitamins and minerals. All fruits and vegetables contain fibre, which helps your body to get rid of waste.

Five a day

Everyone should eat at least five portions of fruits and vegetables every day. You can have them with your main meals and as snacks. For example, you could choose a salad for your lunch and eat an apple or some dried apricots as a snack.

Melon contains lots of vitamins and minerals that keep you healthy.

The freshest fruits and vegetables are the ones you pick yourself.

Eat a 'rainbow'!

To get a good mix of nutrients, try to eat a 'rainbow' of fruits and vegetables every day. This means eating something red (peppers or strawberries), orange (carrots or oranges), purple (grapes or plums), yellow (bananas or lemons) and green (apples or peas).

HEALTHY HINTS

Ask an adult to take you to a farm where you can pick your own fruits or vegetables. The fresher they are, the better they taste!

Meat, fish, eggs and nuts

Meat, fish, eggs and nuts are good for you because they contain lots of protein. Your body needs protein to grow and to repair damage such as cuts and grazes.

Protein in food

Fish and meat, such as salmon and chicken, contain lots of protein. You need to cook most meat and fish before you eat them. Some foods, such as ham and salami, may already be cooked when you buy them.

Try to eat fish at least once a week. The oils in some fish are good for you.

Vegetarian option

People who choose not to eat meat and fish are called vegetarians. Instead, they eat eggs and foods made from plants that contain protein. They include nuts, beans, bread, lentils and tofu.

This vegetarian salad contains nuts, which give you lots of protein.

It's a fact!

Some people do not eat eggs, dairy food, meat and fish. They are called vegans.

Dairy foods

Milk and foods made from it are called dairy foods. They contain fats, proteins, vitamins and minerals such as calcium.

Milk and cheese

You should eat some dairy food every day. You can drink milk or pour it over breakfast cereal. Hard cheese is delicious on its own or grated over food such as pasta. Soft cheese on toast makes a great snack.

Yoghurt is a dairy food.

Too much fat

Some dairy foods contain a lot of fat.
Butter and cream are very high in fat.
Try low-fat margarine instead of butter
and yoghurt instead of cream.

HEALTHY HINTS

Try blending fruit, milk
and natural yoghurt in a
food processor to make
a delicious milkshake.

*Try drinking a glass
of milk every day.*

Fat and sugar

Foods such as burgers, crisps and fizzy drinks belong to a food group called fat and sugar. It is unhealthy to eat too many of these foods. Healthy fats are found in foods such as avocados and nuts.

Healthy fats

You need some fats and oils because they contain important vitamins. These fats are found in meat, dairy food and nuts.

Too much fat

Foods such as biscuits contain a lot of fat. If you eat too much of these foods, your body stores the fat and you become overweight.

Try to eat biscuits only as a treat.

It's a fact!

Sugar clings to your teeth and can create holes called **cavities**.

Fast food such as burgers contains too much fat and sugar. Don't eat these foods all the time.

Sugar

Sugar gives you a lot energy, but it only lasts for a short time. If you do not use up all the energy from the sugar you eat, your body turns the left-over energy into fat. This will make you overweight.

Everyone needs water

Your body needs lots of liquid every day,
as well as food. The best liquid is water.
Try to drink 6–8 glasses of water every day.

It's a fact!

About two-thirds of your body is made up of water.

Try filling a big bottle with water in the morning then drink it throughout the day.

Water

Your body needs water to work properly. It helps you to break down food and keeps the inside of your body moist.

You lose water when you sweat and when you wee. If you don't drink enough water, you may feel dizzy and tired. Feeling thirsty tells you that your body needs more water.

You can get some of the water you need from fruit juices, such as orange juice.

Water in food

Food contains water, too, especially fruit and vegetables. Crunchy foods like celery and cucumber are mostly water. Soups contain lots of water, too.

23

Eating safely

Sometimes food can make you ill. Food stays fresh for a while, but then it starts to go bad. This is because it contains **germs**. Never eat food that smells bad or looks mouldy or rotten.

It's a fact!

Food packets have a 'best before' or 'use by' date. Don't eat them after this date.

The germs in rotten food can give you a tummy ache.

Keep clean

Wash your hands with soap before you prepare and eat food. Wash fruit and vegetables before you eat them. If something you are eating falls on the floor, wash it or throw it away. Keep kitchen surfaces and tools clean, too.

Washing your hands before you eat gets rid of germs that could give you a tummy ache.

Allergies

Some people cannot eat certain foods, such as **shellfish** and nuts. These foods can make them sick or their skin itchy and swollen. This is called an **allergy**. If someone is allergic to a food, they must not eat it.

Healthy choices

A healthy diet is very important.
Here are some tips to make your
diet healthier.

- tap water is as good for you
  as bottled water
- raisins are sweet, but they are much
  better for you than biscuits or sweets
- carrots are healthy snacks

Eating a healthy diet keeps everyone in good shape.

Go easy on the salt

Too much salt can damage your heart. Don't add salt to your food.

Make your own food

Make your own healthy pizzas. Use pitta bread for the base and tinned tomatoes for the sauce. Add your favourite toppings. Include as many rainbow foods as you can. Sprinkle cheese on top. Ask an adult to grill your pizza.

Pizza can be good for you if you use healthy ingredients.

Make a fruity face!

1. Decide which fruits you want to use for your face. You will need something for the eyes, nose, mouth, ears and hair. Ask an adult to help you cut the fruit.

2. Cut a grape in half. Put the two grape halves on the plate, cut-side down, to make the eyes.

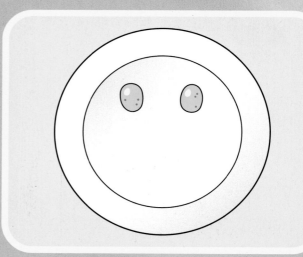

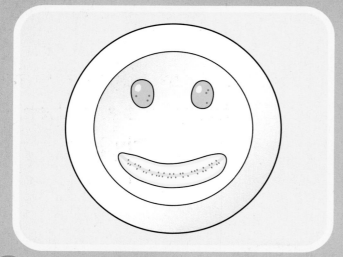

3. Peel the banana and cut it in half lengthways. Lay one half on the plate for a smiley mouth.

28

4. Cut the apple into quarters. Cut one apple quarter in half, so you have a semi-circle shape. Place this on the plate for the nose.

5. Cut the plum in half to make the ears. Remove the stone. Place the pieces on each side of the plate.

6. Now you can have fun with the hair! You could use lots of raspberries, dried apricots or raisins for a curly look.

7. Admire your beautiful fruity face and then enjoy eating your healthy creation!

Eating well topic web

Use this topic web to discover themes and ideas in subjects that are related to eating well.

PSHE
- Taking responsibility for personal health and wellbeing.
- Understanding how to make sensible and healthy choices about food.
- How to prepare healthy and well-balanced meals.
- Understanding that some people eat meat and that others are vegetarians or vegans.
- Pack a healthy lunchbox – try to include some protein, carbohydrates and fruit and vegetables.

GEOGRAPHY
- Understanding where food comes.

EATING WELL

SCIENCE
- How to prepare food safely.
- Understanding food hygiene.
- Why the body needs vitamins and minerals for health.
- Understanding what the different food groups are and how much to eat from each group daily.

ART AND DESIGN
- How to design and make a fun, smiley face from fresh fruit pieces.
- Make a healthy pizza picture! Use vegetables to create a picture on a pizza base.

Glossary

allergy when someone's body reacts badly to substances that are normally harmless to other people

cavities holes in your teeth created by eating too much sugar

cereal a grain crop used for food, such as oats, rice and wheat

diet food you usually eat

energy being able to do physical things

fat a substance in food that contains vitamins your body needs

fibre part of foods such as vegetables that help to get rid of waste

germs tiny living things that may cause diseases

ingredients all the substances that make up a food product

minerals substances such as calcium that your body needs to stay healthy

nutrients substances in food that your body needs to grow and stay healthy

protein a nutrient that provides you with energy to live and grow

shellfish sea creatures with shells, such as crabs and prawns

vitamin a substance that your body needs in tiny amounts to stay healthy

Find out more

Books

Health Choices: Healthy Eating by Cath Senker (Wayland, 2007)

Keeping Healthy: Eating by Carol Ballard (Wayland, 2008)

Websites

This NHS website has excellent information and quizzes about eating healthily:

www.childrenfirst.nhs.uk/kids/health/eat_smart/index.html

Index